E-COMMERCE FOR A DIGITAL NOMAD

E-COMMERCE FOR A DIGITAL NOMAD

A route to location independence

Erik Karlberg

CONTENT

To be a digital nomad.. 1

Put your business idea into words...........................5

Something in, something out 15

Package your offering 27

Let one and one be three...................................... 31

What does the path look like?...........................39

Owner, not CEO 47

Time to become a businessman 57

A brand is born..69

Your store factory..79

The experience of shopping with you.................. 109

Numbers and books 119

To run your company..127

What you have learned 135

TO BE A DIGITAL NOMAD

To be a digital nomad is a dream for many. To be able to travel the world, work from a hotel room before lunch and explore jungles or sandy beaches in the afternoon. To be completely free from going to that office in the morning or reporting to that manager every week. To at the same time earn enough money before lunch to continue traveling. There are lots of ways to find income that can support life as a digital nomad. To write a book is one, to earn money from sponsored content and cooperations via a YouTube channel or Instagram is another. To run an e-commerce business is a third.

Imagine that you can do all your work tasks from your favourite café. The café can one day be in cosy medieval streets of the Swedish summer city Visby, on another day in rainy streets of London. It can also be your very own kitchen table where you sit while snowflakes fall outside your window. Or crawled up in the living room sofa after the kids fell asleep for the night.

We live in a digital world and to be a digital nomad means to digitalise your work life. We no longer have to be standing in a shop to sell stuff, or knock on doors to sell services. Life is online nowadays and so can your career be.

But how do you start a company that can be managed completely location independent? What are the opportunities with e-commerce and is it possible to start small without having to build a warehouse in the living room and run to the post office every morning?

I started my first e-commerce business in 2005. With a few friends, we sold hookahs (Arabic water pipes) to the Swedish market. At the same time we built Sweden's largest forum for hookah enthusiasts. This was long before Facebook, Instagram and YouTube, so working with social media and building a following was something we had to figure out on our own.

Since then I have started a number of companies, one that sold both smartwatches and app-controlled accessories, one worked with staffing for restaurants, one built websites and apps and one sold Apple equipment.

In parallels to my projects and businesses, my day job has taken me travelling the world selling Wi-Fi solutions to telecom operators. I have managed development teams spread out through three continents and participated in countless meetings via Skype from hotel rooms and restaurants during my travels.

My latest e-commerce business is Save Mondays. We are selling a fabric tote bag designed for bringing to the store, not only to bring back from there. Save Mondays was founded as a completely location independent business already from the start and can be managed from wherever there is an internet connection.

However, my driving force to be a digital nomad does not only come from wanting the traveling life. It also comes from being able to stay in my house in the Swedish countryside for work, and not have to spend 1.5 h every day driving back and forth to an office in Stockholm. To be able to work a few hours from my own desk at home, go for a walk along the countryside roads during the lunch break and work in the garden directly when the clock turns five in the afternoon. To drive to the neighbouring village of Järna and enjoy a locally produced coffee at Café Åsgatan 2 at the same time as I'm taking care of orders and accounting. To travel to Beirut for a month during spring, live in a hostel and manage my work while I'm having a coffee at Soul Insight.

This is freedom for me and this can be freedom for you.

E-Commerce for a Digital Nomad gives you everything you need to know to start an e-commerce business you can manage from anywhere in the world. In these chapters you will learn everything from how you can think when formulating and validating your business idea, to how you arrange your warehouse, build your website, manage your accounting and much more.

So pack your bags, it is time to start your adventure!

PUT YOUR BUSINESS IDEA INTO WORDS

Starting a business is easy. To start a profitable business is harder. You, therefore, should start with formulating your business idea properly. A few sentences are enough. By doing so, you will highlight the most important part of what you have set out to start, in what way you will set yourself apart and what it is that will make you succeed. With a clear sentence describing your business idea in front of you, you can reflect on not only if the idea itself is feasible, but also if you believe in yourself as the one bringing it to life. One key to success is to start a business within a market you are passionate about.

In this chapter, you will learn some easy tricks to formulating your own business idea and how to use those words as a tool in your daily work when starting your company.

WHAT IS YOUR PASSION?

Before you write down your business idea, think about what your passion in life is. It can sound like a life-changing question to bring up when doing something as simple as figuring out what your company should be doing, but it does actually have a big impact on the sustainability of what you are about to create.

This is even more important when you are about to start a business as a digital nomad. Managing discipline is so much more difficult when you own both your time and where you perform your job. The closer your company business resonates with your passion in life, the more likely that you will find motivation during those moments when things feel the hardest. And with hardest, I don't mean when you are fighting and sweating with work, but rather when alternative activities crawl up your priority list and compete with your business project. That nice dinner with newly found friends, to mow the lawn or to watch interior design clips on YouTube should all be able to compete with your passion and, most of the time lose against it.

So how do you find your passion? Unless you already know that is. Maybe you spent your life doing horse riding, learned all there is to know about saddles and snaffle bits and now want to help the world by selling a new type of ergonomic saddle made of recycled plastic bottles. But even if you have no clear passion, you have to start somewhere. So what is it that really gets you going in life?

Someone said that we are defined as persons when we are around 10 years old. Our view of the world we have at 10 will remain when we turn into adults. Think about who you were when you were 10 years old. What was important for you then? Which values and interests did you have? Is there anything that you still believe in?

If you want to make it into an exercise, grab a white paper or even better a whiteboard and draw a mind map with yourself in the middle. Make one bubble for each area that interests you and deduct to subareas as you consider and get inspired.

The control question you should ask yourself after each area is can I see myself spend the next three years of my life doing this? Three years of the few years I have to live on this earth. It can seem a dramatic control question, but when you start a business, you have to want to live with it week in and week out for a long time - otherwise, you tire of it. And then it is not worth investing in it. But when you find the right area, the answer will be easy and you will also be the best person to start a business within that particular area.

THE NERD ECONOMY

Our time is one of the most exciting and completely unique periods in the history of humanity. It is the time that all previous development led us by its constant innovation and increased multiplication of ideas. Never before have people on this earth been able to interact with the whole world as if they were their closest neighbour. No matter if it's about politics, the latest TV series or to buy new shoes, the friend we talk to and the store we visit can now be located anywhere in the world.

Imagine a small city center filled with a number of stores. The ones shopping there are the ones living nearby. Imagine what they are selling, depending on where in the world the city is, and when in history it is. In the small Swedish town of Södertälje a number of clothing stores, a single hardware store, the kids' toy store and the food store. In a small village in Jordan, instead a butcher, the car garage and the bakery. A store that only sells caps with prints from 60's gas stations will not live long in any of the cities. Neither will a store selling accessories to racing bikes.

But we live in a different world than what all our parents lived in. In our world, the physical vicinity is no longer a crucial factor to who we hang out with or what interests we develop. Neither does geographical boundaries determine where we shop.

The Nerd Economy is about your target market now being spread out throughout the world, which makes it larger than what it ever could be before. To sell a small set of well-selected products to 100 000 potential customers around the world instead of having to sell everything that the nearest 100 000 neighbours could ever need opens up a whole lot of new opportunities. It even gets much simpler, because knowing everything about a small set of products is a lot easier than to know everything about everything.

Also, the world is nowadays run by nerds and early adopters. If you chose the right niche, your specific nerdy niche spreads to a larger group of people, faster than it has ever done before.

To reconnect to the previous section's discussion about finding your calling, when you finally found your's you can with the help of the nerd economy build something in today's global world that secures your setup as a digital nomad.

WHAT TO SELL AND WHO TO SELL IT TO

The next step of formulating your business idea is to think about what you shall sell and who to sell it to. Maybe you already have a product in mind after the exercise of finding your calling, or perhaps your whole journey started from that you have created a fantastic product you now want to show the world. No matter which, it is time to give some thought about what this product is and who should buy it.

The product in this discussion can be a product or a service you perform or mediate for your customers. In either way, think about what you sell as a packaged product, especially when you will find your customers through digital means.

With product development and the question about selling someone else product or create your own, a later chapter will go through it further.

Let's say you have a product you want to sell. It is now time to do some exercises to get a feeling for if this will work, as well as define who will buy it.

We start with something as simple as the name of what you are planning to sell. The name must reflect what you plan to deliver and be easy for your potential customers to understand. It is also not wrong to give some thought about how the name will behave when people search for it online. For example, if it matches specific words that your customer will type into Google.

The name itself is not important in this stage, but it brings you into a way of thinking - how, when and who it is that will search for your product. It is not enough to have the world's most revolutionary product if the road from a buyer to the product is clear and understandable. The idea of that anything you do on the internet will go viral and spread on its own is unfortunately only an idea. There are many people who put huge amounts of hard-earned money into building apps that they believe will make them millionaires, but only resulted in a few downloads. Or started e-commerce businesses with huge inventories that never moved.

So you need to have an idea of not only who your customer is, but also where this customer will search for the product you sell, and how this person does the search. Even if what you sell never existed before and has no name, you will have to think about which search terms your customers are using when they are open to be exposed to your product. It is possible to completely skip this step, but then it is likely that your marketing budget will have to compete with international multi-million dollar companies - far from the fight that any aspiring digital nomad wants to pick as their first.

It is unnecessary to define the exact name, target audience, ideal customer and marketing budget in this stage. But you should have a few ideas in your head and have given some of it enough thoughts to know how you will succeed with what you are now about to dive yourself into. You must also define a rough market to act within, to have the components for completing what the next chapter is about - your business idea in itself.

YOUR BUSINESS IDEA

Language is a powerful tool to formulate and share ideas and through patterns. It can contain both feeling, logic, definitions and give directions for how new throughs can be formed. By starting in a complete sentence when we define our business idea, we can make sure that it contains the most important aspects when starting our business.

I will sell X to Y and will succeed because of Z.

When you start your e-commerce business as a digital nomad, you don't have to write long essays with marketing analysis, calculations of market shares and detailed launch strategies. On the scale we are talking about for most digital nomads, it is enough to fill in the spaces of the sentence above. Already by doing so you have an advantage over most other companies started every day.

So let us see what we shall fill in in the first part:

I will sell X to Y.

We discussed this in the previous section. It is simply a description of your products and your envisioned customers.

I will sell fabric bags to urban citizens that want to stop using plastic without the hassle, could be the first part of the sentence for my company Save Mondays.

I will sell user-friendly computers to creative people, could be the sentence that Steve Jobs used when Macintosh was created.

Try to formulate your own sentence. It will guide you

and both make you think about and validate your business idea before you invest time and money into your company.

But let's not forget about the end of the sentence, *…and I will succeed because of* Z. It is equally important as the first part of the sentence. You must think through what it is that will make you succeed with your business idea. What is it that will make you stand out from the competition? That you will sustain longer than others and that your customers will shop from you and now someone else?

…and will succeed because I am passionate about saving the climate, could be the last part of the sentence for Save Mondays.

…and will succeed because we combine usability with technology in a way that no one else can do, could have been Steves.

Think about how your sentence ends. Guidance can be found in the chapter about finding your calling earlier in the book. Once you have formulated your business idea, write it down so it is easily accessible (Notes on your phone is a good place for a digital nomad). It is also not a bad idea to print it out physically, draw it on the front page of your notebook in your backpack, or print it and tape it to the wall behind your computer at home.

SOMETHING IN, SOMETHING OUT

To buy something at one price and sell it at a bit higher price is one of the oldest methods we humans use to make a living. Between buying and selling we add some sort of value. In its simplest form, the value is in location and availability, for example, a store where you can buy milk instead of walking all the way to the local farmer. The value can also be to refine goods into a new product or put your brand on someone else's product. In this chapter, you will learn the difference and how to find inspiration to what you should be selling and which value you should contribute with.

SOMEONE ELSE'S PRODUCT

Perhaps the first thoughts that comes to mind when thinking about e-commerce is an online store that sells a collection of products made by someone else. The keys here are collection and the brand of your store. You will have to consider why your potential customer would find their way to specifically your store instead of going directly to the product manufacturer or to bigger and more established stores.

You will also have to think about inventory management and costs related to managing your collection of products. If you build up an attractive assortment you have a good opportunity to create a sustainable business that expands beyond upselling to existing customers. You will also automatically have something to talk to your customers about, both in terms of recurring news about new products coming in and in terms of how existing customers use the products.

When you set up your collection of products, you need to make sure there is a consistency throughout the assortment and that the number of products is both appealing and manageable. It will be easier to build trust and credibility with your customers if you have good knowledge about all your products, compared to if you launch with a collection of thousands of widely spread products.

The value you add when you sell someone else products must also be thought about carefully before you launch. In a global world, your competitors are all just a click away and your credibility is directly measured against big players such as Amazon, Wall Mart and H&M. Your strength as a small player and digital nomad is that you can contribute with more positive knowledge than the big players, and build a personal following around your branding that the generalist competitors will have difficulties keeping up with. Your value does not have to come only from the brand of your store, it can also come from the business model you use. Imagine a subscription service where you get a new pair of underwear in the mailbox every month, or perhaps a subscription of ecological candy on Saturdays - a new bag conveniently arriving in the mailbox every Friday.

If you already have built up a following within your niche, using content on Instagram or YouTube, the value you add is automatically the credibility of yourself as the supplier of the e-commerce site.

Three points to think about when you plan your assortment:

- Product, is it a product I can talk about with confidence?
- Product mix, does the product fit into the assortment, do I create a mix of products that make up an attractive offering?
- Profitability, can I really sell this product at a higher price than what I bought it for?

There is an infinite number of ways to find products to sell. Everything from physically visiting a factory and check out what they've got, to reading paper catalogues or attend trade exhibitions to find the latest products. Luckily even this part of life is being digitalised and nowadays there are really good services online where you can find suppliers of everything from socks to mobiles to dishwashers. The largest service of that kind is Alibaba, a Chinese marketplace for suppliers and factories both from China and from the rest of the world. Use Alibaba to find inspiration for your product mix and to get a feeling of the price you have to pay for your products. Most suppliers you find in Alibaba will only sell to stores and resellers and usually, they have a minimum order quantity of 100 - 1000 units. AliExpress is the little brother of Alibaba and over there, you can find an almost equally large collection of suppliers and products, but priced so you can find single units to buy as a consumer.

You will find more tips about how to use Alibaba later in this chapter.

If your products are available geographically closer, try to visit the supplier or distributor physically and learn as much as you can about the products, as well as what the supplier can offer outside of the specific product you are looking for. To manage fewer suppliers will make your life easier than if every product you sell has to be bought from different suppliers.

YOUR OWN PRODUCT

One way of managing both your calling and to increase your margins is to create and sell your own product. Your own product can be anything from something you manufacture yourself at the kitchen table, to something you hire staff to create or ask a factory to build.

The advantage with your own product is that you can compete using the attributes of the product itself rather than just differentiate yourself using price, brand and availability. You can also charge a higher selling price and get a lower purchasing price than if you are just reselling someone else's product where there already exists an established price model.

The first through that comes to mind when talking about creating your own product is to design and develop something completely from scratch. It can be a new clothing accessory, your own design of a coffee cup or a specific circuit board you make for people building their own lamps. The development and design of your product is something you manage yourself, but the manufacturing you have to either get someone else to do, or work with a method of manufacturing in batches for it to work with a digital nomad lifestyle.

To have someone else manufacture your product can be expensive, especially since most factories require some sort of starting cost to create tools and set up processes for your specific product. Ask around a few different factories when you have a draft of your product design, to get a feeling about what it will cost you. It can be worth it to think a few steps extra about choice of material or adjusting the design a bit if it can reduce manufacturing costs.

The method of manufacturing in batches is when you build your product yourself, but do it in large batches during a limited time. This is the only way your own manufacturing can be combined with being a digital nomad, as long as you are selling physical and not digital products. You can, for example, set yourself up to manufacture a thousand units of that circuit board during the summer, send it to your warehouse and not have to refill until next summer when you build another thousand units. You can start at a smaller scale, but if you want to achieve the total freedom of being a digital nomad and focus on marketing and product development, you don't want to be interrupted by having to build more physical products throughout the year. This method works the best if both the effort and the cost of manufacturing your product is very low, and your margin high enough. If you, for example, can build the circuit boards for \$1 per unit and sell them at \$40 per unit, you can probably be happy with the profit you can make out of a thousand units per year, and it's not the end of the world if a few hundred dollars and some late summer nights are invested in your stock.

Another method to achieve your own product is to start on the other end, which is to use an existing product as a starting point and adjust it to become your own. For my project Save Mondays this is exactly what I did. I started with designing and developing the product completely on my own, built prototypes and made detailed drawings. With this, I went on to Alibaba to find suppliers while I was searching all over Sweden to find local suppliers (of which there apparently are almost none left) that could sew the product I had designed. The answer was most often that the supplier required very large minimum order quantities and that it would become very expensive. And this was after many rounds of first trying to make the supplier understand how the products were supposed to work. It became way too expensive and too big of an investment to build the product completely from my design. Instead I changed my strategy and started from existing products. Here I wanted to build a fabric shopping bag that could be rolled up in a specific way, so I found a supplier of fabric shopping bags on Alibaba and instead asked for the price of modifying their existing product. Immediately it became a lot easier to discuss what I wanted to achieve and easier for the supplier to give me a price for modifications to an existing product when they already knew how much the original product cost to build. The modifications for my project was about attaching a pocket on the outside of the fabric bag, choose the right material for the pocket, put some metal buttons in there and make the straps longer. The main part of the discussion was made by using photos of the original product on which I drew my modifications directly, combined with measurements and choice of materials. The result was a completely amazing product that is both my own and that got a substantially lower purchasing price than had I continued to get someone to produce the bag exactly according to my first design.

In the next section, you will learn more about what you need to think about when discussing with suppliers.

SUPPLIERS AND MANUFACTURERS

Google is really your friend for finding suppliers. For figuring out whether you should work with them or not however, you are completely left up to your own judgment. Especially initially, suppliers and manufacturers will be a vital part of your business. If they don't deliver on time, mess up the quality or use crazy credit terms, your e-commerce success can be hit hard. Therefore, take your time not only to find a supplier but also think and try to judge if it is a supplier you should work with both from a practical and financial perspective.

For selling someone else's products you are often searching for a distributor. Many manufacturers have a list of distributors for different markets on their website and this can be a good place to start. Another way is to just call or email directly to the manufacturer and ask which distributor they recommend for your marked, for example, Sweden or the Nordics. Also, ask if they sell directly to resellers and if you are lucky with a new manufacturer, perhaps you even can get the chance of eventually acting as a general distributor for your market. The simple setup is if there is already a distributor in your market you can apply as a reseller to. Another advantage with that is that the distributor will have related products as well, which can help you broaden your offering by more or adjunct products. When you have applied as a reseller, usually, you will get login credentials to their e-commerce platform for resellers, where you can check out prices and order products. Depending on your company's credit score, you will get different credit terms with the distributor and can use these to order your first set of test products. Some distributors can also act as your warehouse and send the products directly to your customers on your behalf. This is called drop shipping and more about that later in the book.

When you use a supplier from Alibaba, both for ordering their products or ordering that product you designed yourself, there are a few terms you need to know about.

MOQ, Minimal Order Quantity is the lowest number of units that the supplier wants to sell per order. This number is extra important when you ask about your own version of a product they already build. This is because the supplier wants to make sure they cover the investment they have to make in changed tools, new instructions for their workers and still have a healthy margin left. For products in the lower price segment, the supplier usually requires a MOQ of 500-1000 units. When you contact a supplier for the first time to get a rough price, try to mention already from the start how many units you plan to order for the first shipment. Later you can try to negotiate the number down against a slightly higher price per unit, but establish a feeling with the supplier for how much money they will make on you as a customer.

Tips! Negotiate variants instead of lowering the MOQ. For example, ask for a white and a black version within the same MOQ. Usually, it is easier for the supplier to motivate a little extra work on their side, as long as they keep the order value at the same level.

The steps required to establish a relation with a supplier on Alibaba are:

1. Ask for a price of the product, including any changes you want to make.
2. As for a price for a sample, including shipment.
3. Pay for the sample via Paypal.
4. Ask the supplier to adjust the sample according to your comments, pay and get another sample. Do this a few rounds until you are happy with the result.
5. Agree on a contract for the first real shipment, including credit terms, payment terms etc.
6. Pay half the amount (or what you have agreed) in advance via the built-in escrow function in Alibaba.
7. Wait for your shipment to be sent.
8. Pay the remaining amount directly to the supplier.
9. Wait for the final delivery.

You can also start with ordering a sample of the supplier's original product, to get a feeling of the quality and how your own product might feel and look like. The process is the same if you order products without modifications, with the only difference you will probably not need more than one round of samples. However, be careful to always order samples even if you don't plan on making modifications. To feel how the products feel when opening the packaging, how the quality is and how the product works, it's important to communicate with your potential customers with confidence.

Ask the supplier to send you photos throughout every step of the process, to follow the rock from remote. It is especially important when they are completed with production and are about to send the shipment. Contracts and payments are managed within Alibaba, even if most suppliers want to get paid for specifically the samples via Paypal. Most often suppliers market free samples in their listings, but my experience is that they instead charge enough for the shipping to cover the cost of sending the sample or prototype.

Tips! Make it very clear with the supplier who will pay for the final delivery once the goods have reached your country. It is easy to promise that shipment is included, but only to the nearest seaport and not all the way to your door or warehouse.

PACKAGE YOUR OFFERING

To make both your customers and yourself understand what you are offering and what problem you are solving in exchange for their money, you should offer it properly packaged. For a company to be easy to understand is key to the time required to convince anyone to purchase something from you. It is even more important in an e-commerce business, where the goal is to enable your customers to both find you and be convinced to buy from you with minimal manual interaction.

SUCCESSFUL PACKAGINGS

The most successful companies in the world are all extremely good at packaging their offerings. Some to a degree that devoted and loyal customers will even envision and speculate about how new products will look like, even before they are released. Apple is a clear example of this, but also companies like Adidas are extremely good at packaging what they are offering.

Packaging is about making it simple for your customers to reach a purchasing decision. Don't make your customers make a lot of decisions about your offering before they purchase. If your product requires customisations, make sure these are required after the customer has completed the purchase.

The example with Apple is simple, they have clearly separated product segments that the customers have been trained to recognise. The customers already know from beforehand about the difference between an iPhone and a MacBook, and once they browse apple.se they will quickly reach an option to purchase.

Services are normally harder to package since they contain a larger portion of uncertainty about what will actually be delivered. Especially services delivered as man hours.

YOUR CLARITY

One way of looking at packaging is to see it as a scale, where one end is a white paper and the other a standard product that can be ordered with one click. The white paper gives your customer complete freedom to decide and define what they want to buy from you. This is always done with you and works just fine if you are selling hours of consultancy within your area of expertise. However, it doesn't work as good if you are trying to start an e-commerce business where you are selling wooden coffee cups or if you want to scale up your web agency to sell to more clients than your old employer.

The purpose of packaging is not to completely say no to inquiries that go outside of the template you are trying to fit your customers within, but it gives both you and your customers a common language to use as a starting point. Packaging is also a way to inform your customers about at which level you are expecting them to purchase from you.

If you are selling physical products, think through how they are packaged both in categories and collections as we discussed in earlier chapters, and how they as individual products and groups of products are packaged in the eyes of your customer. The wooden coffee cups, do they have a name that sounds right and are they sold individually or in a pack of four cups that fits your customer's home perfectly? If you are selling individual cups, will it be worth the hassle of dealing with packing, delivery and returns? It could be better for both you and your customers to only sell them in packs of four.

To sell services is as mentioned earlier more of a challenge for packaging. However, it doesn't mean you should avoid doing the packaging, on the contrary, it requires you to think a few steps further. To package and define your services are especially important when selling them through an e-commerce channel. For a web agency as in the example above, packaging and productifying services can give your customers an important indication about which price range you expect your projects to be within. If you, for example, package a feasibility study for a new web site with a number of tasks you will perform at $3 000, your potential customers will not expect a fully developed web site for that same price.

So packaging is not only your tool to position yourself on your market, it is also a tool to position your offerings in relation to each other.

LET ONE AND ONE BE THREE

Now that you are on the way to start your own e-commerce business and start your life as a digital nomad, the most important thing to consider is that the business you start will be profitable as soon as possible. To have a short path to profitability is not only a financial question, it is also a question of sustainability in what you are about to get yourself into. If the business already from the start is set up to take a long time to reach profitability, it will hurt every day on the way there. If it has low costs, high margins and a short path to profitability, the journey will be much more enjoyable.

FIXED COSTS

It is easy to get carried away when you are enthusiastic about your new product and business idea. Especially when you have done the numbers and see a short path to profitability. And this is good, it is important to keep inspiration high. However, it is very important to make a sober analysis of your fixed costs before you start off.

E-commerce is, by nature, something that need not have expensive fixed costs. There are no requirements on a physical store with expensive rent and you have no opening hours where you must pay salaries to staff to keep the shop open. However, there are many traps to fall into, where expensive fixed costs are hidden. Your own warehouse, staff that packs and ships, expensive e-commerce platforms or contract with marketing agencies are traps to look out for.

To start an e-commerce business as a digital nomad means that you as soon as possible want to reach a point where you can head off to where you yourself want to be. And for this to happen, you cannot have a business where your cash is slowly being eaten by fixed costs.

In a later chapter, we will go through how you can keep your fixed costs down by using 3PL (third-party logistics) and to hire services instead of personnel for the otherwise expensive functions such as customer support.

A health level of fixed costs is that they are not fixed, but instead follows your success closely. When success is there you have all the possibilities to renegotiate with suppliers by increasing your fixed costs in exchange for higher margins.

Tips! Make a spreadsheet where you enter all your fixed for your business and envision a scenario where you are not selling a single item. How many months can you endure without putting in more cash? How many months can you endure by putting in more cash from another income you have?

MARGINS

No matter what your business is about, you must have healthy margins in what you sell. Healthy does not always have to mean high, but as a newly started e-commerce business not backed by millions in marketing budgets, learn to develop a phobia towards margins under 30%. When you have established this phobia it is time to recall what we said about packaging. To make your business sustainable, each sale must give you enough money for it to be worth it.

"To be worth it" can include a whole lot, but some of the most important points are:

- If a customer is not happy, can I afford to send out a new item without losing money?
- Can I give a really nice discount?
- How many items to I need to sell if I give one to a YouTuber?
- Can I let an unhappy customer return an item without having to argue about details and blame?

One guideline is to make sure that each sell via your e-commerce business gives you more than $10 of margin and that you can give away every fifth item without going under. You should not plan to give away every fifth item and hopefully you will not have to, but it will make it easier initially if you can give away products for marketing.

If you are selling electronics, only resell digital products from other or in any other way stumble into products with low margins, it is extremely important to analyse your business model in light of the above. Even if you are envisioning a storm of orders, things will not be like that initially. To have the possibility to use a discount code or give away a product to get those new customers in, can be crucial. Also to give a good discount to an unhappy customer, or to positively surprise another with accepting a return and paying back the money with no discussion.

Also consider that tied-up cash also costs money. If you, after all, sell products with low margin, make sure to avoid having to deal with warehouse and stock. Neither by yourself or by paying for a third party. If you are selling other companies' products (could be with your own profile, for example, t-shirts with your own prints but delivered directly from the factory), make sure that everything that has to do with customer support and returns are handled by your supplier. It could be easier to motivate a lower margin if you are selling digital products, if the effort for delivery and keeping the customer happy is kept to a minimum.

YOUR TIME

One factor that many people forget when starting their first business is to include their own time as an expense. It is even so many entrepreneurs see their own time as a cheap asset to be used to increase profitability of the company. Check ads for local restaurants and coffee shops for sale and you will find many examples of descriptions about "perfect opportunity for an owner who can work himself". Unfortunately, this is a hidden signal that the business is being run with such low margins you will have to put in free or very cheap labour for it to be profitable.

The goal of being a digital nomad is not to put in lots of hours into your business at a low hourly rate. It would kind of remove the idea of striving for freedom. The goal for your own e-commerce business is that you yourself will eventually be the most well-paid person per hour in your company.

You must put in lots of non-paid working hours into your e-commerce adventure both at the start of it and once it is up and running. And even when you have a successful e-commerce empire you will still work way too much compared to the salary you pay out to yourself. But the important thing is to not design and calculate your budget for this to be the case.

With the coffee shop, don't invest your money in the business if you can't see an opportunity to at least step out completely from the day to day operations. What you add to the operation of the business needs to be your passion and your interest, not time in the form of manual work. With your e-commerce business, make sure that you have designed your operations so all tasks can be outsourced to others. Never build something into your operations that requires your specific time and presence. We will talk more about this in the chapter about Owner, not CEO later in the book.

Your business is not profitable until you either can get really good pay for your time or can afford to outsource all the services required to operate the company. Every day until then will require lots of effort from yourself on every level of the company, but remember that profitability is not reached until after that.

Tips! Make a spreadsheet where you try to estimate the time required to operate your company for each role. Put in the number of hours per week that your marketing manager would have to spend, how many the finance person would need for the accounting etc. Then put a cost on each hour that covers a reasonable salary for yourself. And by reasonable, I mean you should be able to calculate with an hourly salary of at least $50. Then compare with your sales budget and calculate how much you would have to sell per month to both pay for these hours as salary, and still have a healthy profit margin left in the company.

WHAT DOES THE PATH LOOK LIKE?

For every idea you get when taking a shower, or when you wake up during the night and have found the solution to the world's every problem, you have to know the path. The path is not only how your idea will get itself from living in your mind to a materialised product or offering, it is also how this product or offering will get in the hands of your customers and how their money will get into your pocket.

AN IDEA DOES NOT HOLD VALUE

There are many people who have had an absolutely amazing product idea that will disrupt markets and change how we live our lives here on earth. There are few people who actually bring this product to life and even fewer that succeeds in changing how we live our lives.

Knowing how to code in the early times of Apple's App Store for iPhone meant a steady stream of friends and acquaintances who felt the smell of financial freedom in creating apps. They brought one idea after another for apps that would revolutionise the world, to the coder they wanted to build their idea. I am all for creativity and always glad for all attempts to shape the world for the better, but there was always something missing with these ideas. They all assumed that the idea would make customers all over the world pay the $1 and make us all rich. The idea was also often valued so high that the time it would take to develop it, no matter how much effort it would take, would only mean a share of around 20-30% of the venture. The effort from the person with the idea would be to tell the coder about the idea and keep 70% of future revenue, with no further investment in either paying for the hours coding or in any marketing. What was missing was an understanding of the path. The understanding that there needs to be a clear path was probably easier to grasp in other lines of business at this time, since the App Store had a gold rush shimmer around it, where the dream of immediate financial success was too tempting.

The point of the comparison with how to deal with ideas for apps is that even when working with apps in the App Store the path must be clear. How does the potential customer find their way to what I am trying to sell? Can the first customers purchase be used to spread knowledge about the product to others? If so, where and how do we find enough initial customers to get things going?

An idea does, unfortunately, not hold any value. An idea is only a thought that needs to be materialised into something to gain value. Maybe the idea cannot be materialised, but can be a foundation for another idea that, in its turn, can be materialised and turned valuable.

EXECUTION IS EVERYTHING

To take your idea from something you dream about at nights into something that actually exists in reality holds different levels of difficulty for different people. For some, it is easy to throw themselves into the execution and get something working within a few days, and others require years of preparations and considerations before taking action. No matter which one you are, you will soon reach a point where you must give your idea some structure.

We humans have a more practical side than what we sometimes want to admit. We like to touch, feel and smell things. Use this to quickly reach a point with your idea where you can touch, feel and smell it. It can be in writing down product descriptions, make a draft of an invoicing template or to actually make a physical of digital prototype of your idea.

When I started with Save Mondays I began with a lot of theoretical thinking about how a fabric tote bag could be modified to make it easy to take it to the store, not only with me back from there. Closely after I had the idea of rolling it up, I went to the local grocery shop and bought myself one of their fabric bags to test my idea. The first test was made with some pieces of normal paper and a few needles and the second test was made using fabric from a torn pair of jeans combined with my old sewing machine. By making a working prototype, it became easier to both imagine how the product should work and look like, and easier to show to friends and family what I was up to.

If you are planning to sell others products, order samples as early as possible. Feel them and try out what you are planning to sell properly. It is not only good for your own knowledge about what you are about to sell, it also brings you one step closer on the path to execution.

But not even bringing your product idea into life or collecting an assortment of cool items to sell back home on your couch is a full execution of your business idea. It is not until your first customer, someone who you didn't know from before, both finds their way to your shop, gets interested in what you are selling, places the order and are happy when the product is delivered, that your execution is complete.

MARK YOUR PATH

It is easy to believe that business is just about getting to know your customer and delivering something this customer wants. That is, however, to make things a bit too easy for us. To be successful in business is all about getting to know your customer's customer. The one who stands behind your customer or the forces that are there to push your customer in the direction where they will purchase something from you.

Pen and paper are one of the most effective tools we humans have innovated. Total creative freedom in a simple format. Use them also here, when marking your path for your product or service. Start as far away from your own store as you can and write down a trigger or a need. Then draw a small line and add the next one. Don't mind that each trigger or need is not in the same category or type, just add them to create a long chain of triggers and needs.

For Save Mondays the first trigger or need could be the law that stipulates that all stores now need to charge for and inform that plastic bags are bad for the environment.

Law against plastic bags -> Fabric bags at $3 -> Environmental concern -> Comfort -> My customer -> Google for a solution -> savemondays.se -> Order a pack of 3 -> One in the car, one in the purse -> Bring Save Mondays Fabric Tote to the store -> Fill with groceries -> Unpack at home -> Roll the bag up again

Try to mark a few different paths for your project. You

will have good use for them not only when considering if your project will actually work, but also later when you need to adjust something to reach more customers or when your market prerequisites change.

It is also important that your path doesn't stop where your customer purchases something from you. You need to also have a direct understanding about what your customer will actually achieve; its what they buy.

Tips! Make your path more alive by drawing balloons for every step where you add speaking quotes that illustrate how the thoughts are formulated at that step. "Do you want to buy a bag?", "No thanks, I have mine with me".

OWNER, NOT CEO

As a small business owner, it happens easily that the company is built too much around yourself as a founder and owner, that everything has to go through you. It is natural when we build something, we are keen that our vision for the company shines through everything and that our invested money is used in the best possible way. To delegate and give control and responsibility for parts of your company to others is hard to do and usually, this becomes a problem as the company grows and employees are added to the operations. It is also something that you as a founder and owner perhaps postpone thinking about until that growth has been reached and you have a few employees.

However, to succeed as a digital nomad and e-commerce businessman, you must think differently already from the start. As difficult as it might be, you must strive to not be part of the production of what you are selling. Always strive for taking the role as only the owner of your company, not as an operational CEO.

Your operational CEO should instead be digital.

BE A SMALL DOG, BARK LIKE A BIG DOG

Larger corporations are organised with owners, board of directors and a CEO responsible for the daily operations. Below the CEO many employees execute the daily work. The owner of a big corporation does normally not interfere with picking orders, marketing or finding new products. They will rather think about a general direction for the company, get reports about how things are going and between that mostly be concerned about the returns that the investment is making. As a location independent businessman, you should strive to reach that role. You will to some level have to be both CEO, marketing director and warehouse worker, but these roles should only be an exemption from your target role as owner. To reach there you have to be smart and make use of both automation and buy services you otherwise would have performed yourself.

Design your company to work as if it was one of the largest in the country, even if you are the only person working for it.

List down all roles that your business needs to be operational. Then go through every role and ask yourself: in which way can this role be digitalised or performed by someone else than me?

To see examples, these are the roles involved in Save Mondays:

- Product manager, responsible for finding new products.

- Marketing manager, defines and plans campaigns.
- Content manager, takes care of communication in social media.
- Logistics manager, deals with the warehouse, optimises how to deal with deliveries.
- Warehouse worker, picks orders, sends deliveries, deals with returns.
- CEO, coordinates everything above and deals with any issues.

The product manager is the one spending time in Alibaba, writing requirements and designs new products. This role is difficult to digitalise, but we should anyway consider the thought. Is it possible for new products from our suppliers to automatically end up in our shop? Or can we instead create a routine out of this role, where we once per month spend just one hour adding new products?

For the marketing manager, we need to set up a few boundaries and define some campaigns initially. However, with Google AdWords and Facebook Ads we can outsource much of the ongoing work to their software. What we need to let the marketing manager role define manually is a budget and an offer we know works, the rest we can leave to Google and Facebook to manage. For Shopify, that we talk a lot about in this book, there is also a function called Shopify Kit that automatically suggests campaigns and marketing actions for you based on your content and products.

To manage the content on social media can so far not

be completely automated while keeping integrity and authenticity. However, here is a good role to make use of a virtual assistant, or pay someone to help updating your social media feeds. You will get very with a good set of photos and clear instructions on how you want the language to sound like.

By using a third party supplier for your logistics we can reduce most logistics managers' daily work. The only thing remaining is to keep track of the stock levels and order more when it's time to refill. And even this you can automate when you are starting to feel comfortable with it, just configure your warehouse to send an order directly to your suppliers when the stock levels reach a certain threshold.

The tasks of the warehouse worker also end up at the third party logistics supplier. They will most often deal with returns and let you know what came back. If you combine the warehouse outsourcing with a virtual assistant where you instruct how the communication should look, you have managed to free yourself completely from the role of warehouse worker.

When using a software as a service platform for e-commerce such as Shopify, you will not have to put much effort into maintaining the web on a technical level. There will be work before launch setting everything up and some period of fine-tuning after, where you will adjust the minor details and wordings. But after this, the platform and theme you have selected will manage itself.

As a CEO, you have a never-ending to-do list with tasks

for your business and maybe it is a utopia to reach a level where even the CEO is automated or digitalised. But that shouldn't stop us from striving in that direction. Make a habit out of now and then doing an analysis of what you are putting time into for your company, and ask yourself again how you can delegate this to a virtual assistant. When your one-man company is managing both sales, logistics, marketing and customer interactions while you are sleeping - then you have reached your goal.

BUILD YOUR VIRTUAL TEAM

Luckily you are not the only one with ambitions to become a digital nomad. This exists all over the world, so there are many specialists and generalists eager to sell you a few minutes of their time online. Helped by these people, you can build your virtual team without having to sign up for expensive running costs.

Go back to your list of roles required to run your company and go through the ones where you haven't yet been able to automate the role completely. The next step is to see if you can purchase the role from a virtual assistant instead. A virtual assistant is someone you hire online to help you with manual tasks or to fulfil a specific role. Tasks for a virtual assistant can be everything from extracting reports from your e-commerce platforms and summarise the numbers into a new report for you, to be responsible for all support enquiries. The good thing with having a business with English as the main language is that it is possible to find virtual assistants all around the world available to help even with customer-facing tasks. But don't stay away from using virtual assistants even if your customers speak a non-English language, there are many tasks within your company that can be managed by a virtual assistant anyway.

If you need a local language virtual assistant, please check local Facebook groups or ask around in the neighbourhood if a student wants to make some extra money helping you out.

To find international virtual assistants there are some good web services that provide both a marketplace and payment methods for hiring your assistant. These are a few starting points:

- Fiver
- Upwork
- Freelancer

Search for virtual assistant and you will find many potential new colleagues. When you have found someone interesting, act as if you would have hired the person as an employee. Even if it is a small task you need help with, you should have good chemistry with the person and that you feel you can hand over areas of responsibility to this person with confidence. It is only when this works you can scale your business by delegating tasks to a virtual assistant. Perform a couple of interviews with the potential virtual assistant via Skype. Remember to use video as well and not only audio, it is always a lot easier to feel the chemistry if you can see each other. Also check references and reach out to previous employers and clients to learn how the person cooperated in real projects.

Once you have secured one or a few virtual assistants, it is time to write down extensive work orders for the tasks you expect them to complete. Store these in a good location and see that your virtual assistant is completely in sync with what is written in the documents. These work orders are the tools for you to delegate as much as possible of your own work to the virtual assistants. Don't be afraid to delegate responsibility to limit the number of times that a task must be run through you. For example, if your assistant is managing returns, give him or her a clear mandate to approve returns up to a certain value and only report a weekly or monthly summary of how many were returned, instead of having to contact you to approve every return value. Take a calculated risk for this delegation and adjust the approved levels if needed. This will make your business self sustained already from the start by having automated processes built-in and you will not be swamped with tasks where you are the only one that can make a decision.

TIME TO BECOME A BUSINESSMAN

This thing with starting your own company can seem frightening. There is a lot of talk that it is expensive and difficult to start your own company. And not to speak about the risks involved. But if you only have some routines in place, it's not that dangerous.

In this chapter, we will go through the practical pieces of starting a company. The goal is to have a company that can be both the sender and receiver of your e-commerce transactions, and that is as separated from you as a person as possible.

INCORPORATE

There are many books and texts written about forming your own company. A lot focus on advanced company and tax formation setups. For your needs, aim for the simple and easy way. Find a setup you can manage on your own (or via a virtual assistant) and most important a setup you can manage online. Remember that you want to be free to travel and live where you want, not where your tax authorities require you to be to fill out some papers.

If you are in Europe, consider checking out the Estonian e-residency and services from xolo.io. They provide an all-digital experience with integrated company setup, tax reporting and bank account - Especially made for digital nomads. Once set up, you can connect your payment providers from your e-commerce platform and get your accounting automatically taken care of through their online tools. The company itself will be formed within the EU zone with you as the full owner.

In the US, there is a similar product from Stripe called Stripe Atlas, where they provide a package for a straightforward company setup process. In the background, a C Corporation in Delaware is formed, and Stripe takes care of filing for Tax ID and all the other paperwork. They also set up a Stripe account as part of the process, allowing you to quickly accept payments from your customers.

For your local country legislations, aim for setting up a limited company that can live as it's own identity. This will make it easier for you if your digital nomad adventures would take you to extended stays in another country where you would need to, for example, change your taxation setup.

Tips! If you are incorporating in your own country, consider setting up a holding structure for your business already from the start. This might sound contradicting to keeping things simple, but a holding company can help you keep better control of your tax situation when living outside of your home country. It also gives you the possibility to invest in other revenue-generating projects or companies, while keeping the exposure to the holding company instead of yourself as a taxable person. For the simple digital nomad incorporation packages mentioned above, it is, however, still difficult to arrange the holding setup.

BASIC INFRASTRUCTURE

When you have incorporated your business, there are a few things to get running before you can use the company properly.

To get money into your account, you need a bank account. By using one of the company formation services mentioned, you will automatically have gotten your company a bank account as part of the formation process. If you formed a local company in your home country, you hopefully also set up your bank account as part of the process. Having a credit card connected to your company account for expenses will make things easier for the accounting, but also consider using your personal credit card for expenses to collect some personal kickback rewards on the way.

No matter who your customers are, you need to be reached over the Internet and therefore need a good domain name. You probably already have a good idea of which domain name you want, after searching for a name for your company. So then the only thing remaining is to purchase your domain and connect it to your email. Your website can come in a later stage. I usually buy my domains from a local Swedish supplier, or through Godaddy, through which you also can easily manage all your domains.

For the email, most suppliers of web hosting or domain registration also provide a basic email service. Often this service is good enough, but I prefer the whole package where I can use calendars, contacts and notes without hassle with all my devices. Therefore I usually use Google GSuite or Office 365, which both are around €5 per month. There are also some free options available from players such as Zoho with their Zoho Office. However, the simplicity and convenience of Google's or Microsoft's services make them a better option, at least for me. When all is set up, you can easily add your email supplier to any iPhone or Android device you use, and also reach the very same services through gmail.com or office.com. To connect your newly bought service from Google GSuite or Microsoft Office 365 to your domain name, they provide detailed instructions within the administration section of each service.

Another important part of the basic infrastructure is the accounting. To have this in place already from the start is extremely important to get all routines in place and to have full control over how the company is doing at all times. There are multiple services available to manage your accounting online and you will find some advice on this in the chapter about Numbers and books. The most important thing is to have a system in place to record all accounting transactions and also from the same system be able to send out invoices, when required. I use a Swedish service called Bokio, where I can handle both accounting, invoicing and salary payments from within the same system.

Also have a good infrastructure for files and documents already from the start. Even if it is only you working with your business initially, hopefully that fact will change one day and you need to invite others to share what you are working with. Therefore use a service for file storage where several persons can reach and work with the same files. I usually use Dropbox or Microsoft OneDrive for this purpose, but other services such as Box or Google Drive can also be used. Using a file sharing service not only gives me the possibility to share files with others, but it also gives me a sense of security and safety that my documents are stored in more than one place (at least both at Dropbox or Microsoft and in my two computers at the same time). It also makes it easy to share individual documents or complete folders with others. Dropbox will give you 2GB of storage for free and you can get more space either by inviting others to the service or paying for a higher subscription. With all free services, there are limitations though, for example, Dropbox has a limitation to how many devices can be used with their free account. Using a paid service like Google GSuite (with Google Drive) or Microsoft Office 365 will remove the hassle of these limitations.

A last and also important part of the basic infrastructure is to have a good system for to-do lists for the company from the beginning. Use the built-in features of iPhone (syncs perfectly with your Mac via iCloud) or Google Tasks. I use the app Things that is available both on iPhone, iPad and the Mac. No matter which solution you choose, make sure that you can schedule tasks to show in your to-do list on a specific date. This will help you create reminders for important events and tasks such as when you need to file your tax reports.

As you can notice, we use cloud services for as much as possible also for the basic infrastructure of the company. The reason for this is to lay the foundation for a company you can sustainably manage as a digital nomad. It shouldn't matter if you lose your laptop or just don't want to bring it with you. You should be able to reach everything and manage your business from any computer, phone or tablet anywhere in the world.

Tips! Create a note in Notes on your phone where you put all the basic information about your company infrastructure, so you can easily reach it when you must provide it to suppliers or customers. In this note, you should keep information such as Tax ID, bank accounts, formal and full company name, registered address for the company and bank account number in international format (including IBAN and BIC, which you can get from your online banking service).

GET YOURSELF A FEW MUSTS

The dream of living as a digital nomad is in itself a dream of getting away from musts. Because of this, it can sound strange to get oneself more of these musts already before starting. It is however, very healthy both for your company and for yourself as a digital nomad to get the habit of regularly checking in on how things are going.

So no matter the type of company formation or formal incorporation setup you choose, I recommend that you appoint a board of directors. If your company is a limited liability one, this will come naturally and be the same as the formal board of directors. If not, ask a few friends and family members if they can support your business by joining this board. The role of the board is not to fiddle with the daily operations of the company or to take on tasks related to developing the business, but to check in on and follow up. Agree with your board you meet up quickly every second month via Skype and create a standing agenda for these meetings. By doing this, you force yourself to both work in a structured way with your company and to lift your eyes towards the horizon even during times where the inspiration and motivation are not as strong.

Example of such an agenda can be:

• Sales walkthrough, reporting on the development since the last meeting.

• Product development/new collections, what is coming up.

• Marketing, overview of what has been done and a general note how the plan is forward.

- Finances and reporting, go through available finds and show that reports to tax authorities have been sent in.
- Status of the boards to-do list.
- Next meeting.

Make this meeting as formal as it needs to be. If you are running a company type that requires formal minutes from board meetings, create these from each meeting. If you are running another company type, it might not be as formally important, but for traceability, you should do it anyway.

Tips! Create a common to-do list for the board where you add things you agree on during your board meetings. Trello is a great service for creating work that flows in a very simple way using the model of post-it notes that are moved for each completed step of change of status. Try it!

NAME

To figure out what to call your company can be a difficult question to answer. If you are starting simple without the full incorporation, just make sure that the name you plan to use doesn't conflict with existing company names or trademarks and you will probably be fine. But for registering an official company, such as a limited liability one, authorities could look into your name suggestion thoroughly to make sure they can give your name the same protection as other companies.

Since you are starting an online business, you probably want to start by searching for available domain names that would suit your upcoming business. Some company registration authorities recommend that you don't purchase any domain name before your company name is secured, but I recommend that you actually start from available domain names when you plan for what to call your company. Also, the formal name of the company need not be exactly what you use for a domain name, or even the name you use for your online store. But it adds to your credibility in the eyes of your customers if the name on their receipt at least closely resembles how the store where they made their purchase is represented.

Finding a name can happen in many ways and perhaps you already have a name in mind. Unfortunately, many good names are already taken by an existing company or some trademark, so it can require some creativity to find a name that works for you. One method of finding a name is to work with lists of associations. The method consists of writing down all words and synonyms you can think of for your business in a long list. You then make combinations of these words to get to a new list of possible names. You can also combine the same words with general words such as geographical words or perhaps your own name.

When you have found a name you like, it is time to go through your own validation process:

1.   See if the domain name is available. You want at least the .com to be available, and if you target a specific market also the top level of that market, for example, .se for Sweden.

2.   Google the name to see if it appears in some strange setting, or if it means something dodgy in another language. Try out variants of the name, including adding an s at the end and use both singular and plural forms.

3.   Check if the name is available as a username on social media platforms such as Instagram, Facebook and Twitter.

4.   Search company registration databases in your country for similar names.

5.   Search the European database of trademarks, EUIPO, for similar trademarks.

To search for domain names you can simply use the search function at your domain registrar, for example, Godaddy. The reply will be if the name is available for a number of top-level domains. If you are looking for a domain name in a specific top-level domain that is not available through your normal registrar, you can try to direct your browser to NIC.topleveldomain, for example, nic.io for domains under .io or nic.co for domain names ending with .co.

To check if the name is available as a username on social media the easiest way is to just try to reach the profile via facebook.com/YOURNAME, twitter.com/YOURNAME etc. and see if you find any existing profiles.

Once you have a name you like and have verified, it is time to send it in as part of the company formation process. Usually, you have to send in at least three suggested names, so make sure you have three good options or variants of your preferred company name available.

When I registered the company for Save Mondays I had to send the registration back and forth to the Swedish company formation authorities a couple of times. Some of the names that they didn't like were Save Mondays AB (conflict with a similar trademark) and Trevligare E-handel AB (something like "nicer e-commerce", too general for their liking). Eventually, they agreed to the name Smond AB. So my business is presented under the name Save Mondays from the domain name savemondays.se, but the company itself is called Smond AB.

A BRAND IS BORN

There is something almost magical about brands. A simple name, a logo and a way of communicating that every day grows into a more solid identity. An identity that almost becomes an individual in itself.

You now have the task to let your very own brand be born and grow into its own identity. It can sound epic and almost overwhelming, Especially when reading about the millions that big corporations spend in brand work such as just changing a logo or a color. But the good thing for us is that we start off from an empty paper.

NAME

You already did most of this when you selected the name for your company. When it comes to the name within your brand, you need to take it one step further and think about how you will use it.

Should the name be written in capital letters, separated or joined, pronounced in plain English or with an accent? Will it be shortened or get itself a nickname?

Also try to put your name together with your products, feel the format when you pronounce it.

Save Mondays Tygpåse (Save Mondays Tote Bag)

"I bought a tote bag from Save Mondays"

Save Mondays sells tote bags you bring with you to the store, not only back from there

Tips! If you want your name to work in different languages, try to let your computer read it out with text-to-speech in that language to verify how it will be pronounced.

LOGO

The day you have a logo for your company, that is the day when you breathe life into it for real. You will feel it in your whole body you are about to create something real when you have taken this important step towards creating something with its very own and free-standing identity.

To create a logo can be everything from very simple, cheap and quick to extremely complex and expensive. How good the result is doesn't necessarily have to do with the cost level, even if creating one yourself is not always recommended.

If you have a tiny feeling for graphics and design however, it can be both rewarding and interesting to give it an attempt yourself. If not, I suggest that you purchase the service of creating one.

Purchasing a logo can be made in many ways:

1.   Generate a logo via an online service. Shopify, the e-commerce platform that we will talk more about in this book, has a free service you can use to create your own logo online, https://hatchful.shopify.com.

2.   Order the service of drawing a logo from a designer online. Through services such as fiverr.com and upward.com, you can find really good designers from around the world that are both highly skilled and willing to draw you a logo for a small amount.

3.   Turn to an established agency. The result will be good, but a lot more expensive. If you have a friend that is a designer at an agency, or have some services to swap for design work from an

agency, you might get away a bit cheaper.

Some advice if you want to try drawing your logo on your own:

• Use fonts and combinations of fonts as a foundation. Google Fonts have a huge selection of free fonts and a tool with which you can try out each font with your own words or company name.

• Give proper attention to the details, make sure that the padding between graphical elements is calculated and leave nothing to chance.

• Use the golden ratio for all distances and proportions, to make sure your creation is easy on the reader's eye.

• If you want to have symbols or icons in your logo, begin with using a similar image found on Google. Once you feel that the symbol is a good fit, draw your own version of the image based on the one you found, to make sure you don't inflict on someone else copyright.

Once you have your logo in place, have a few different production-ready files available in your Dropbox or Microsoft OneDrive for easy access from anywhere. You will need to have a number of different formats easily available.

• Horizontal in black with transparent background.
• Round version with covered or transparent background.
• Square version with transparent or covered background.

Tips! Don't be afraid to use several versions or types of logos in your brand work. Maintain a common theme, but it doesn't necessarily have to be the exact combination of text+images in all versions.

LANGUAGE

How your brand communicates is another factor to think about when you define the brand. If it has a happy and casual style, or a more formal. If the brand uses a personal voice, or communicates using the voice of a company mascot.

Try to write down a few sentences with the style of language you choose. Try with writing an example post on social media, since this and via email will be your mail channel of communication that your customers will see.

Even the language choices you make is good to put down into a document. This makes it easier to both remind yourself and to show others how you expect them to work with your brand.

BRAND PROFILE AND COLORS

It is easy to skip the details of finding a color schema and choose which fonts to use for your business when starting small, but these small details give your brand a whole new level of professionalism if you just put a small amount of effort into it. And it is not even difficult.

When it comes to fonts, go to Google Fonts and find at least two fonts you think goes well with your logo and type of business you are setting up. You will need at least one font for headlines and another for plain text, but it is not wrong to have an additional one to use in banners and other graphical elements. Be inspired by how other successful brands work with fonts. Download the fonts you choose from Google Fonts and both install them on your computer and put them in a folder on your Dropbox or Microsoft OneDrive så that you have easy access to them.

To choose a color scheme is also something where there is a lot of science and research available, but where we can make use of existing tools to not have to learn all this science ourselves. Coolors is one such tool where you can generate colors that look good together. With the generated colors, try to imagine roughly how they will be used. For example, imagine one of the colors being for your headlines, another for links and maybe the same for buttons, etc. Save the colors by making a screenshot from the tool, or write down the color codes.

The result of your work with fonts and colors needs to be made accessible both visually and as files. Create a document using Word or Pages and type some example headlines using the font you selected, and write out the name of the fonts. Also, add a few squares in the document with the colors you selected and add the color codes in both HEX and RGB format. Also, paste your logo into the same document using the different formats you created, and you suddenly have your brand profile ready to use, both for yourself and to be shared with others.

SOCIAL MEDIA

Register and set up profiles on all the big social media when your name is decided. Add a logo and some profile photos so it looks solid and finished. After this, you don't have to work actively with all channels, but at least you have secured the name and made sure to be there for the future.

Even if Facebook is something of the past by some, especially when looking at how younger people use social media, it is still an effective channel for both marketing and interaction with your customers. Have a Facebook page registered for your business and use it both to reach out with sponsored posts and for recurring updates about your company and the are you are active in. An important detail of Facebook usage for e-commerce is the Facebook Pixel. It helps you target customers that have visited your website before. We will go through the pixel in this chapter.

Instagram is a great channel for e-commerce businesses selling things. You can reach and inspire your potential customers to shop in your store both by building your following through talking about your calling and by using sponsored posts.

Twitter as a platform has become somewhat political and is suitable mostly for brands that take a clear stand in political or social issues and wants to take an active part in the debate.

How you use social media results directly from how you

defined your business idea and how you interact with the marked path you identified earlier for your product or service. While you use your social media and communicates using your brand, it will also grow as its own identity and by adding time to the equation you will find the most devoted followers that will come to love your brand and what you stand for.

YOUR STORE FACTORY

To make your life nomadic and free as a digital nomad, you must build your business as a factory. The vision to aim for is a business completely automated and requires no hands-on interactions by you. However, this is a vision, so it is perfectly ok not to reach all the way there.

In this chapter, we will go through the tools to set up your store factory and make it produce sales.

YOUR WAREHOUSE WITH SOMEONE ELSE (3PL)

One of the success factors of successfully running an e-commerce business as a digital nomad is that you don't manage the warehouse yourself. Somehow it is pretty self-explanatory, if you plan to be location independent you don't have that many possibilities to drag around a bunch of stuff to each place you visit. Even for the digital nomad who doesn't travel outside of their own kitchen, it is still not recommended to manage the warehouse yourself. The reason for this is not to put your valuable time and energy into tasks such as picking, packing and shipping when you can put the same time and energy into working with your marketing and develop new products.

The concept of letting a logistic company manage your warehouse is called 3PL, third party logistics, and there are a number of suppliers who offers services for this.

Warehouse suppliers

Many warehouse suppliers can offer 3PL services, both locally in your country and internationally. However, most have a price level that requires volumes hard to promise as a newly started e-commerce store that should be lean enough to be operated while traveling around. In this section, I will go through some realistic alternatives you can start with already before growing your business into a giant in your field.

Amazon is the omnipresent corporation that sells everything from digital music to electronics, interior design goods and food. Amazons key to success when starting was a unique and optimised warehouse management process. The simple idea was to store each item in the warehouse not based on category or name, but based on which items their customers usually bought together. Amazon was one of the first actors to use Big Data to optimise their operations. As their own marketplace grew, they also let others sell through amazon.com and as a next step even allowed these sellers to rent space in their own warehouse and make use of the unique warehouse management process. No matter if you sell through Amazon or through your own channels, the advantages of letting Amazon manage your warehouse are many. Amazon also has warehouses around the world, so if you are based in Europe you can put your goods in their outlet in Germany. Their pricing model is both per sent item and a monthly fee per square foot. You activate the service by adding the feature to your Amazon account, create your products in their system, and after that, send your goods to their warehouse. The smoothest way of selling your goods from the Amazon warehouse is by selling through Amazon itself, but it is also possible to integrate other software directly towards the warehouse. If you are selling in the US market, for example, Shopify has a very easy to use integration towards the Amazon warehouse.

The service from Amazon is called FBA (Fulfilment by Amazon).

PAYMENT

Perhaps the most important function of all companies is one of receiving payments. To both accept payments and manage them in a convenient way will therefore be one of the most important cornerstones of your store factory.

The limit-of-shame for all e-commerce with payments is the ability to accept credit cards. Above this, a plethora of payment methods make things even easier for your customers. And the more of your customers favourite payment methods you support, the more likely that they will give you their money in exchange for your products.

Stripe is a payment provider with a different focus than many others, they have focused really hard on a smooth and user-friendly journey for their end-users and for the developers that want to use their platform. It is also very easy to set up an account, add account numbers for fund transfers, etc. The advantage of that Stripe put so much effort into making it easy for developers to use their service, is that all e-commerce platforms have built-in or ready-made plugins for Stripe. This is also the case for Shopify, which I will show you more about when I describe how you set up Stripe. Stripe has no monthly fee and only charges a percentage of each purchase made through their platform.

Stripe manages both Visa, MasterCard and American Express. They also support Apple Pay, which works all the way through to Shopify and gives the user an amazing experience.

A simple account with Stripe without any history larger operations with them will give you a transaction fee of 2%. You can reduce your transaction somewhat fee when you increase your payment volumes. Besides the transaction fee from Stripe, some specific credit cards add an additional small fee.

Paypal is one of the incumbents with payments online. They have been around for many years and got their breakthrough because of the simple way they offered for sending and receiving money with just an e-mail address as recipient. Paypal has also meant a lot for international payments for everyone shopping those unique items on eBay from a strange country, or from a small enthusiast that sells things directly of their blog. Even if being an old player in the game, Paypal has in some markets received an uptake in the last couple of years, since they have again focused more on usability, a new app, etc. In your project to start an e-commerce business, you might also need to pay for samples from suppliers you find through Alibaba and similar marketplaces. For these, the norm is to use Paypal for initial payments. To accept Paypal payments in your store is very smooth, simple and costs nothing per month other than the administrative time required to make sure the transactions are recorded in your accounting software. And the small percentage that Paypal charges for each transaction.

To set up Stripe

Stripe is easy to set up and you do it directly on their website. You must give them some details about your company and also send them a scanned copy of your passport, so they can verify that you are who you claim to be and that you are authorised to sign contracts for your company.

Once you have registered your account with Stripe, you are ready to accept payments using credit or debit cards either manually directly through their online tool, or through any of all the e-commerce platforms that integrate with Stripe. Including Shopify.

To integrate Shopify with Stripe you will find the settings under Settings and Payment providers, where you add Stripe and follow the simple instructions to approve the integration between Shopify and Stripe.

Stripe as a machine in your store factory

Payments with Stripe are seamless for your customer. They will shop in your store, put their items in the shopping cart and continue to payment with little notice to the payment going through Stripe. In the background through, Stripe is handling everything that has to do with card payments and Apple Pay. This means they take care of all the hustle of credit card payments, including managing things like 3dsecure (when redirected to your own bank to approve the transaction via password or SMS).

Payments via Stripe will work like this in your store factory:

1. Your customer places an order in Shopify (your website)

and pays with a debit or credit card.

2. Through Stripe, your customer will enter their card details or approve the payment with Apple Pay. No details about the card are managed outside of Stripe.

3. The money is allocated on the customer account and an order confirmation e-mail is sent out.

4. Once the order is fulfilled and the items are sent, the allocation will be converted into an actual charge to the customer's account and the money ends up at Stripe. You can see the details of this by logging in to your account with Stripe.

5. The next day, Stripe initiate a transfer of the collected funds to your bank account.

6. A day or two later, the money ends up on your bank account.

After this, your items are both sold, sent and you have received payments with no manual interaction from you with payments.

You can configure how often you want the payments from Strip to happen. To make your bookkeeping simpler it might be a good idea to configure them to be sent once per week or once per month instead.

MARKETING

The purpose of talking about your operations as a factory and to free up time from things that can be automatised and turned into a machine in that factory, is to give you time and energy for product development and marketing. Your digital marketing requires you to set up a number of different suppliers to start with. You will then learn what works and what doesn't, and adjust your machine to eventually become a well-oiled machinery that also produces marketing.

With **Facebook**, you can advertise either as sponsored ads of different types within users' social media feeds, or as classic banner ads next to the feed. Your ads in the feed can be pure text ads or be combined with photos or short video clips. They also have direct product ads that make the target user end up directly within your purchasing flow if they click the ad.

All ads on Facebook requires you to have a registered page as the sender. You also need to create an account in Facebook Business Manager. To this account, you will connect a payment method and provide information about your company. You can then create ads from the tool Ads Manager, where you also configure limits for how much to spend on your campaigns, define the target audience and lay out how the ad will look on different platforms.

To get started with Facebook advertising, you need:

1.   A Facebook Page for your company, product or service.

2.   An account in Business Manager for your company.
3.   A debit or credit card to pay for the ads.

To make your advertising via Facebook become a part of your store factory, you need to configure one or several ads you run continuously. This is done by creating an ad in Ads Manager and configure it to be run without an end date, but with a limit on how much the ad can cost you every day. These options are configured under the budget and validity section of the ad.

A concept good to know about for advertising on Facebook is the Facebook Pixel. Have you noticed that directly after you have visited an e-commerce website, your whole Facebook experience is filled with ads from that specific store you just visited? This is made possible by the Facebook Pixel. It works by a small piece of code on the e-commerce website that reports a user's visit and behaviour back to Facebook. This information is used by Facebook to trigger showing ads specifically targeted at these users. This method is highly effective since a user that has visited your website is already much more likely to purchase from you than anyone that hasn't visited the website. Therefore this method has become very popular and is used by most e-commerce merchants.

To use the Facebook Pixel, you need to install it within your e-commerce platform. For Shopify, there is a guide available from within Shopify Kit that helps you with all steps necessary to set up the pixel and create targeted ads for it. You can also easily just ad the pixel code within the settings of your Shopify store.

Google is for most people almost the same as the internet. It has lots of implications that one player is so dominant in our online life, but for marketing it is hard not to relate to this giant company. Google has a wide variety of advertising products. They supply everything from the classic text ads on top of search results, to ads on other people's websites, to ads within their own product search and within YouTube videos.

To get started advertising on Google, you need to register an account for your company with Google AdWords. The first time you register, you will go through a setup guide to set up your first ad. Payment for the ads is handled by a debit or credit card you configure for your business account in AdWords.

Advertisement with Google (at least the classic format) is based on specific search terms. You choose several keywords where your ads will be shown if users search for anything using these words. Once a user sees your ad and clicks on it, you will pay the fee of that specific keyword. The fee differs from word to word. Popular words such as "fashion" or "gold" will cost more per click than more unique words where the competition is less from other ad buyers.

In Google AdWords, you can configure a maximum price for each keyword, limiting how much you want to spend on each click. You will also choose an overall budget per day you want to spend. The algoritms of Google will base on this buy views for the words you have selected and deliver views and clicks to your configured ads. You can also make additional adjustments about your target audience and make Google show the ads only for potential customers in Sweden for example, or perhaps only for people searching for a specific word from the city of Washington.

The possibilities are endless and a whole industry works with optimising and finding the right path for advertising with Google. You can, however, set yourself up for a good start by testing yourself and learning the basics. Google will suggest default values for most settings to start you and you can adjust them as you learn more.

Tips! As a general guideline, always start small and measure your results when working with digital marketing. Spending 10$ should not only get you views and clicks, it should also give you valuable insights into how well that specific target audience responds to the message of that ad.

THE STORE ITSELF

A company with the business idea to do e-commerce wouldn't be much of a company if there wasn't an e-commerce store to start with. Luckily there are no reasons to build an e-commerce store completely from scratch nowadays. Unless your business idea requires such revolutionary flows and interactions from your customers that no one have done it before. But even then you should first have a look at the existing platforms and see what can be solved by expanding their functionalities with plugins and apps.

What you need in an e-commerce platform is a service that gives you the tools to host a customised web page with features for a product catalog, shopping cart, purchase and order management. Since you have the advantage of starting your business from scratch, you will hopefully not have to put a lot of effort and energy into integrating with existing systems and web sites. But even this you can do with most e-commerce platforms.

Most services for hosted e-commerce also contain features for information pages, blogs and sometimes options for managing newsletters. These features can also be handled via a standalone website for your company, or by using additional online services, but using what is in the e-commerce platform you chose will give you a shorter time to go market.

In this walkthrough I have focused on platforms and services with a reasonable price level for a newly started e-commerce business, that can be managed by a digital nomad. There are platforms that charge a lot more both for setting up and operating the store, but they often require deep analysis and pre-studies before you can even get started. There are also an almost infinite number of services similar to the ones I mention here, but they are usually from smaller players or targeted at specific local markets.

Shopify is as you will notice in this book my favourite and therefore the service we will go through with most details in this book. The strengths of Shopify is the solid foundation that anyway gives a high level of freedom to adjust the store experience using themes and to expand functionality via apps. Apps are something that have made Shopify grow even more due to the ease of which a merchant can add new features. Apps are available for everything from selling digital products (e-books, music downloads or similar) and subscriptions to integrations with legacy systems and marketing channels. Shopify has become very popular among everything from small businesses being run from the living room to large international brands that have built their e-commerce solutions using Shopify. The platform is completely cloud-based and cannot be installed on your own servers.

The first store running on Shopify, and the reason Shopify was created, was the founder's snowboard business. From that time, they have grown into managing e-commerce for everything from hobby projects to big players such as Red Bull, Tesla and New York Times. Shopify has a wide variety of payment providers pre-integrated and it is easy to get started with Paypal and Stripe payments, as we discussed earlier in this chapter.

To get started with Shopify is easy and they even offer a free period of two weeks when you don't have to pay for the service. Once you have registered an account, you will get access to your admin interface, where you configure everything that has to do with your store. When your free test period has expired, you will need to enter a credit card for your account so that the fees from Shopify can be withdrawn properly.

Shopify charges a fixed monthly fee (at the moment $29) and a percentage on each order processed by the platform. The percentage level differs depending on which level of subscription you choose, but starts at 2% and goes down to 0.5% for the highest subscription level.

As a newly started e-commerce business, there are just a few things you need to do to get started:

- Choose a theme and work on adjusting it to your look and feel.
- Configure taxes and shipping.
- Verify terms and conditions and other texts.
- Add your products and images.
- Configure payments.

You will need to spend some evenings putting some love into your store before it is time for launch. Try to add your products and get a feeling of how they are presented using the theme you selected, with photos and describing texts. Adjust until you are satisfied and ready to show it to your first customers.

Shopify has a feature to password protect your store and this is a great way to work on your store until you have everything in place. You can share the password with friends, colleagues and perhaps even with your first test customers. On the day of launch, you will remove the password protection and let both customers and search engines in to look around.

In the next chapter, we will go through more about how you can create a unique experience for your e-commerce store.

WooCommerce is a plugin for the enormously popular webb and blogg platform Wordpress. With WooCommerce you can extend your existing Wordpress installation with features for e-commerce and integrate these features into your existing web experience.

WooCommerce has a wide range of plugins available and also has the advantage that plugins can be created independently by a payment provider without having to be approved by a central organisation. This does , for example, make WooCommerce have a better integration with unique payment providers such as Klarna, than Shopify.

There are also a lot of plugins from WooCommerce themselves, for example, to sell digital products, subscriptions and memberships.

Setting up WooCommerce requires a bit more effort than with a platform such as Shopify. But if you feel comfortable working with Wordpress or have a colleague with the skills for it, WooCommerce is a good choice.

The steps required to get started with WooCommerce are:

1. Install Wordpress on a server you have control over, or at your web hosting provider.

2. Choose a Wordpress theme compatible with WooCommerce.

3. Download WooCommerce from their website.

4. Upload the WooCommerce plugin to your Wordpress installation and activate the plugin.

After this, you can adjust Wordpress and WooCommerce to an e-commerce experience you are satisfied with.

Wix is an online website editor that can easily create websites of all kinds. The tools available via the Wix editor allows you to create everything from a simple blog to a more advanced e-commerce store. The starting point is always from a website and it's design, so you will start by adding a store section to your website and will then be presented with settings for e-commerce. Via the editor, you can decide where the list of products should be shown and also add products listed. Once the store section is available on your website, you will have access to the e-commerce tools from the Wix settings. To accept purchases, you need to configure taxes, products and payment gateways.

Wix supports both Paypal and Stripe as payment gateways and to use them you must be on one of their premium subscriptions for e-commerce.

You can find Wix at https://wix.com/ and a basic subscription for e-commerce starts at $17 per month.

Squarespace is another online website editor that can create both your website and your e-commerce shop. The tools are easy to use and both the interface and the resulting website is clean and solid. By adding commerce features to your site, you can publish a section where you showcase products and allow your website visitors to purchase them. Squarespace supports payments via both Stripe and Paypal and a wide number of currencies.

You can find Squarespace at https://squarespace.com/ and a basic subscription for e-commerce starts at $26 per month.

The tips about customer experience in the next chapter is valid for any platform you choose to power your store.

ACCOUNTING

Accounting and bookkeeping are some of the most boring things with running your own company. Having papers, receipts and invoices in order just to type them into complicated software isn't what most people want to spend their time doing. It is also considered difficult, since it is easy to make mistakes and many people instead hire a consultant to take care of all this.

There is a number of really good web services that can make it both more fun and easier to manage your accounting yourself. To a certain extent, tasks can even be automated and a lot is happening around this at the moment. In a few years, you can definitely manage the accounting from your e-commerce business as a completely integrated part of your automatic store factory. Until then, let's try to get as close to automation as possible.

Suppliers of really good digital services for accounting starts to pop up as mushrooms from a moist lawn, and accounting consultants that can help you both in a traditional paper-way and digitally, can be found in every small town and in every block. In this walkthrough I have focused on some of the most interesting and established digital services you easily can get started with and where there is help to be found both from the supplier and from others using the services.

Freshbooks is a service originally targeted at consultancy firms that sell time by the hour. The interface is really smooth and you will have an easy time figuring out how to create estimates and proposals, track spent time and use all this to generate invoices to your clients. However, Freshbooks also does accounting and helps you out with keeping track of your taxes, so it's a great tool to also integrate with your e-commerce platform. By integrating with platforms such as Shopify or WooCommerce, you will automatically get all transactions from your e-commerce store imported into Freshbooks. Combined with the large number of integrations towards bank accounts (and PayPal), you can then synchronise all transactions in your company. Freshbooks also have features for expense management and incoming invoices, so these can also be handled within their simple interface. The only thing missing from Freshbooks is payroll management, but once you have grown your business to include employees you can expand by integrating with other great services such as Gusto.

Freshbooks can be found at https://freshbooks.com/ and starts at $15 per month for their smallest subscription.

Gusto can be found at https://gusto.com/.

Xero is a full service for running your company online. It has a professional feeling and you can use it for everything from keeping your books in order, to issuing quotes, invoices and keeping inventory of the items you sell and sorting out expense claims. It also has built-in functionality for managing payrolls, but can also integrate with Gusto for a full payroll service. For syncing your bank statement with your bookkeeping, Xero offers a bank reconciliation feature that lets you match rows in your bank statement with invoices, payments or expenses within Xero. There is also an add on module to manage projects within Xero, with billable time and all that you need to run a consultancy firm. One thing worth exploring with Xero is their App Marketplace, where you will find a wide range of extensions and integrations with other online services. The App Marketplace you will find integrations with most e-commerce platforms, for example, one for Shopify from Bold.

Xero can be found at https://xero.com/ and starts at $9 per month for their smallest subscription.

Shopify Integration by Bold can be found at https://apps.shopify.com/xero/.

YOUR FACTORY FLOW

Once you have your store factory in place it is time for it to work to create both sales and manage deliveries for you. To wrap up how the factory flow holds together, let's follow the flow using some examples.

A potential customer sees an ad for your product in Instagram and clicks the link to your website

•　The ad on Instagram is managed manually using Facebook Business Manager.

•　You configure a budget of a few tens of dollars per day the ad is shown.

The potential customer reaches your website and end up directly on the purchase page for the product

•　The page, product information and the whole purchase process is handled by Shopify.

•　The look and feel and graphical profile has been adjusted to your company by editing the theme of your Shopify store.

•　Product images and descriptions have been uploaded by defining products within Shopify.

The customer adds the product to the cart and continue to checkout and payment

•　Shipping options and fees have been configured in Shopify to match what it costs (or what you want to charge) for you to send the products.

•　Payment options have also been configured in Shopify for the suppliers where you have an account and a contract, for example, Stripe and Paypal.

The customer is sent to the payment flow of Stripe

• The money is withdrawn from the customer's debit or credit card and are stored with Stripe.

• When the customer reaches the confirmation page within your store, Shopify marks the order as complete and awaits delivery.

• You receive an email notification about that an order has been made (can also be received by a push notification in the Shopify app).

The 3PL supplier fetches new orders for fulfillment

• The warehouse management system from your 3PL supplier fetches all new orders from your Shopify store.

• A picking list is printed based on all new orders.

• Staff at the 3PL supplier picks the items for each order.

• Staff at the 3PL supplier makes each order ready and hands all deliveries over to the shipping supplier, while marking each order as sent in their system.

• The warehouse management system updates each order in your Shopify store with information that the products have been shipped.

• The customer gets an automatic notification via email from Shopify that the products have been sent.

The products are sent to the customer

• The products are sent with whichever shipping supplier the 3PL supplier works with, and that you have a contract with.

• A notification is sent to the customer that the shipment

has almost arrived.

- The delivery reaches the customer a day later.

The customer fetches the products from their mailbox or from the shipping supplier

- Depending on the size of the package, the customer either receives it directly in their mailbox or have to fetch it from an office of the shipping supplier.
- The customer picks up and uses the product.

The money arrives at your bank account

- After a day, Stripe transfers the funds to your company bank account.
- The fees from Stripe have already ben deducted from the transfer.

An email notification is sent to the customer two weeks later

- An automated message formulated as a personal email from you as the store owner.
- The customer is thanked for the purchase and encouraged to leave a review on your website (or any other review service).

Another email notification is sent to the customer a week later

- An automated message formulated as a personal email from you as the store owner.
- The customer is reminded to follow your company in your social media channels and also receives a good discount for their next purchase.

- The discount code is created in Shopify and gives, for example, 50% discount on the next order.

By the end of the month, accounting information is sent to your accounting service

- A sales report for the last month is extracted from Shopify and imported into your accounting software.
- A transaction report for the last month is extracted from Stripe and imported into your accounting software.
- Can be replaced with integrations and apps, check what is available on the Shopify App Store for your accounting software.

Tips! Make a drawing of your whole store flow as a flow chart. It will be much easier to explain and understand your operations if you have a clear diagram to start from.

EMAIL

The communication foundation of the Internet is still very much alive and thriving. Email addresses are natural ways to share a communication channel between companies and their customers, but email also works very good for sending out newsletter, automatic notifications and for communication between different systems. The direct interaction with customers happens more and more via Instagram, Facebook Messenger, chatbots or through iMessage (Apple has a company version of iMessage as well). But the automatic communication and anything more formal, still happens mainly through email.

To have your factory rigged to accept and deal with any incoming emails, set up a number of different addresses where communication from the outside world can be directed. This is the first step to also delegate handling these addresses to different virtual functions within your operation, so think through which addresses and functions you can make use of in the future.

Some basic addresses you should have set up, with examples from Save Mondays.

• hello@savemondays.com is for general questions and reach outs from customers. The address is shown on the website, on business cards and in any communication with customers.

• invoice@savemondays.com is for all services and suppliers that send invoices via email.

• erik@savemondays.com is my personal main address and is always used as the sending address, to make a non-personal inquiry into a personal interaction when the email hits the customer's inbox.

The personal main address is the account identifier with the email supplier, while all other addresses are aliases or groups (depending on what your email supplier will call them) that their simplest form just forwards all incoming emails to erik@savemondays.com. When parts of your store factory are outsourced to virtual assistants or specific services, these forward settings can easily be replaced with a shared inbox that several people can access, or just by forwarding to the email address of your accountant.

Email is also used for sending out confirmations of orders, information about that the order has been sent and a number of other automatic messages. Make sure that also these have a clear but personal language to increase your customer's ability to connect even closer with your brand. You can configure exactly how this communication should look like via your e-commerce platform.

With Shopify, it is also possible to add functionality for sending out delayed messages to encourage more sales and enhance your customer relations. One message could be an email that asks the customer how they liked the product and encourages them to send in a review, that is sent out two weeks after the order was delivered. Another could be to send another thank you email four weeks after the order, with a discount code for the next purchase. If you formulate these messages in the right way and also follow up manually with each reply you get, you can actually build in customer relations into your factory without too much work. At the same time you will get both valuable feedback coming back, and hopefully a couple of new orders as well.

Email suppliers

In the old days, the company that gave you your internet connection was also the company that provided their customers with an email address, both for personal and business customers. Nowadays, there are a bunch of alternative options to explore. For the email handling, I recommend that you choose a supplier that gives you a complete package with email, calendars and contacts. Be extra careful when exploring the options with the company where you bought your domain name, or with your internet service provider, they sometimes offer old and inflexible solutions.

With **Googles** tools for email, calendars and contacts you basically use the regular Gmail, but with your own domain name. They also have quite a few other services under the GSuite brand - everything from chat to websites, all of Google Docs, etc.

Google GSuite works good with both your Mac, PC, on the web and in your phone no matter if it's an Android or iPhone. To easily access your email via any web browsers by just entering gmail.com is handy. Even what you write in Notes on your iPhone can be synced with your account at GSuite, so you can access them from all your devices (notes is not as early accessible via the web though).

The price model for GSuite is that you pay around €5 per user and month. You can however create as many aliases and groups as you like under your domain, so when you start small you don't have to pay extra for addresses such as hello@YOURDOMAIN or support@YOURDOMAIN:

GSuite is found at https://gsuite.google.com.

Being the mother of all email solutions with their infamous Exchange platform, **Microsoft** is not far behind Google for offering web services for email, calendars and contacts. With Microsoft things work basically the same way as with Google GSuite, you set up an account and pay around $5 per month to access your services via office.com.

An advantage with the Microsoft version is that it is possible to add a few dollars to include licenses for the full Office suite as well. With this, you have the possibility to download Word, Excel and Powerpoint using the same account on office.com. For both the email and Office licenses there is a package for around $12 per month.

With Office 365, Microsoft has also established a reseller network, so you can purchase your account either directly from Microsoft or from some other supplier you might already have a relation with. One such example can be your domain name supplier. When you choose your Office 365 package, be careful to select the version that includes Exchange functionality, so you won't buy the one that only contains the Office suite and no possibilities of connecting your own email with your own domain.

You will find Office 365 on https://office.com/.

As I mentioned earlier you should check twice that the email service that **your domain name or web host supplier** offers you is complete with calendars and contacts as well. Also, make sure that it will work seamlessly from all your devices. If it is mentioned that the service is an IMAP account and nothing is mentioned about calendars and contacts, it is most likely a simpler service that will work but will limit your productivity.

Some suppliers will offer Office 365 as an alternative for their customers. By signing up for Office 365 with an existing supplier, you can collect multiple services in one invoice and avoid having yet another payment relation to Microsoft or any other email supplier.

There are a number of providers of platforms for newsletters, but **MailChimp** is one of the better ones. With MailChimp, you can easily set up an account for free, build an audience and send out nice-looking newsletters with their built-in templates and tools. The free version allows you to collect up to 2 000 subscribers and once you have reached that limit, you hopefully already have enough profit in your business to pay for the next level. Once you have registered with MailChimp you get access to an easy to use tool where you can manage your lists of subscribers, monitor statistics from your campaigns (how many subscribers received the email, how many opened, how many read) and also create new campaigns and newsletters.

One advantage with MailChimp is that it is easy to create forms for your customers to register for the newsletter, that you can use on other websites and services. If you have an existing blogg you can simply set up a form that encourages your readers to join the newsletter. You can also create specific landing pages, that can also categorise the subscribers registering so you can manage them separately. One example use for this can be that if you run a campaign on Instagram you will always refer to a link in your bio that leads to one landing page, where your customers can fill in their email address to have the chance to win a product by the end of the month.

You will find MailChimp on https://mailchimp.com/.

THE EXPERIENCE OF SHOPPING WITH YOU

That your business lives in a digital world doesn't mean you can ignore how your store looks like, how your staff greets your customers and how you follow up and give great service to your customers. It is even more important in a world where reviews and recommendations have gone from being a thing between friends, to be systematically collected in marketplaces and comment sections.

Now and then go through the whole experience of shopping with yourself, to see what you can improve and make smoother. The force of positive surprises is also something that you should have in mind, it is the small details that will make your customers choose you, follow you in social media and tell their friends that your store is the place to shop at.

In this chapter, we will go through the parts of your store operations that directly integrates with your end customer. From how your ads are created to usability, how quick your page is loading on the first visit to how the bags look like that the items are delivered in. They all give you great opportunities to communicate your brand at the same time as you build trust and relations with your customers.

THE SHAPE OF YOUR STORE

The most obvious part with the experience is the storefront design and layout itself. We have earlier in the book talked about the e-commerce platform Shopify and I will use the very same as an example here. However, the same points apply also to other platforms.

The first impression that a potential customer gets when they shop with you is not, as one might think, the store itself. It often comes much earlier, already when the potential customer interacts with your brand in their Facebook or Instagram feed, or via an ad they see somewhere on the web. Therefore it is important that also ads are constructed with a design language that the customer will both recognise and get a good impression from.

Once the customer has landed in your store, their first impression will be based on how beautiful it is. If the store falls easily on the eye and have colors, images and logotypes of high quality and professionalism, we have won the customer over half ways to trust. Language shall also not be forgotten. Make sure that all your texts are webb worked through and do not contain spelling or wording mistakes.

If you get all these points under control, you are on a good way with your design:

• Professional logotype that works well with the background that it's shown with.

• Consistent use of fonts and colors.

• No placeholder texts due to lack of content.

- Good product photos that clearly shows what you are selling.
- Distance and white space between design elements that falls easily on the eye.

It is however not only the design and graphical layout to be right for your customer to decide that it is safe and worth it to shop with you. Your site also must be designed so your customers know exactly how to find the next step to proceed through the shopping experience. Usability and predictability should work to your advantage, not against you. Unless you have a revolutionary idea, use well-established metaphors and features that your customer will recognise from other e-commerce sites. A shopping cart and to have a meny with those three bars that is easy to reach on the mobile, are both well-established features you should rather mimic than try to invent yourself. Try to, as far as it is possible, reduce the number of choices that your customer must make and use default values wherever possible.

When you put together your website and reach the state of testing it, also perform your tests with a slow mobile phone and also using a slow internet connection. Things that can make your website slow is if you use images of too high quality or use an external service that slows things down. If you develop your theme at a coding level you will know these things yourself, but if you use an existing theme and experience slow loading, check your image sizes after upload as a first step.

What you are trying to achieve with both the layout of your website and with optimising the speed of which it loads, is that your customer should feel safe enough to put their money under your care. This is even more important when you have just started your business and haven't been able to build up any trust yet. To further enhance the feeling of safety, there are a few more things you should have control over.

- Make sure your website uses SSL (encrypted traffic).
- Make it very clear which payment methods you accept and offer at least one where it is clear for the customer that they don't have to give you any of their details, such as PayPal or Klarna.

When using Shopify, a major part of the layout and design of a store is realised in a theme. A theme contains HTML code that defines how the store looks like when opened on a laptop, a mobile or a tablet. Each theme has several features that can be customised directly via the administrative interface of Shopify, but you can also customise the theme on a coding level if there is anything more advanced that you need to change. All the free themes you can access through Shopify are all well adjusted to make your store both look professional and easy to use for your customers.

Tips! Shopify has a service for royalty-free photos of very high quality you can use for your store and for marketing material. Check it out at https://burst.shopify.com.

ENHANCE THE EXPERIENCE WITH APPS

Apps in Shopify are a way to enhance your store with additional functionality that either Shopify themselves or a third party developer has created to improve the platform. These apps can be everything from functionality to synchronise inventory with Amazon fulfilment services, integrate with Google product listings or give the merchant tools to group products so the default Shopify platform doesn't support. Most other e-commerce platforms also have some sort of app setup, but Shopify has the largest and most mature ecosystem with their app store.

Apps are available both as free and as paid versions and prices are usually around $9 per month. You will find the apps in the Shopify App Store (https://apps.shopify.com) and can install them directly from there into your store.

Build a newsletter

In the previous chapter, we talked about MailChimp as a supplier for your newsletter platform. For Shopify, there is an app that integrates directly with MailChimp, which makes your customer email addresses automatically sync over to your newsletter audience list, and also allows you to encourage visitors not yet customers to sign up for your newsletter.

The cool thing about MailChimp is also that you can categorise your contacts so you can send targeted newsletters. It is easy to target a campaign only towards customers that already have bought something from your store, and another campaign targeted towards those who only registered without yet buying anything.

The MailChimp app för Shopify is free and you will find it by searching for ShopSync in the Shopify App Store.

Keep your existing blog

If you have an existing blog, you can integrate it with Shopify instead of publishing your content twice, or having to cancel everything you built up before. By using an app to automatically import the content from your existing blog, you can continue blogging just as before and your content will automatically end up within your new e-commerce website.

The app for importing blog content costs around $6 per month and you will find it by searching for BlogFeeder in the Shopify App Store.

Group products

If you need to create groups of products, or sell bundles of, for example, three fabric bags for a lower price than for one by one, you need to have an app to keep your inventory in order. With such an app you can create a new product that contains other products. Just be careful to also represent your new grouping product in your warehouse, so your customers will actually receive one pack-of-three items instead of receiving three individual deliveries.

The app for bundling products costs around $10 per month and you will find it by searching for Bundles in the

Shopify App Store.

Remind about abandoned carts

To automatically remind customers that put items in the cart, but for some reason didn't complete their purchase, is a very effective way to increase your sales. The reason your customers didn't go through with the purchase could be they didn't have their credit card at hand, or that they hesitated to spend the money in that moment.

The functionality to remind your customers about abandoned carts is not an app but is built into Shopify from the start. You will find customisation options for the feature under Settings and Checkout, where you can decide how the email should look and how long the system should wait before sending out the message, for example, one, ten or 24 hours later.

Automatic bookkeeping

There are a number of apps available to integrate Shopify directly with your accounting software. These two will start you.

• Xero Integration by Bold for Shopify can be found at https://apps.shopify.com/xero/ and integrates your Shopify store with your Xero accounting and business tools.

• OneSaas offers a module for integrating your Shopify store with your Freshbooks account and can be found at https://www.onesaas.com/integrate/shopify-with-freshbooks/.

AUTOMATE YOUR COMMUNICATION

All communication that goes out from your company helps building your brand and deliver the image of you and your company you want your customers to have. This is also true for any communication sent out from software, or that is automated.

This is an area where you easily can differentiate yourself and make a good impression compared to other stores. And this without even spending too much money or effort.

Just put some time to go through all the messages being sent out from your e-commerce platform. Make sure that the wordings fit your brand language and there is a personal tone in the communication that makes your customers feel well looked after.

Tips! If you configure your automatic emails to come from something other than noreply@yourdomain, for example, yourname@yourdomain or hello@yourdomain, you immediately encourage your customers to just hit the reply button to contact you. This opens a door for talking to your customers instead of closing one in an almost hostile way, which the noreply@yourdomain approach can easily be experienced as.

By integrating with platforms such as MailChimp you can also create advanced flows of your communication.

For example, you can create an email automatically sent to your customer seven days after they have completed their purchase, where you thank them for their purchase and encourage them to follow your social media accounts. Another message can be sent out three months later, where you send along a discount code for their next purchase. By working with these messages you not only continue to build out your store factory, you also caress how your customers experience shopping with you.

NUMBERS AND BOOKS

We have earlier gone through some services that you can use to manage your accounting online. It is however not enough to have that service in place, you also must keep track of the numbers you put in there, make sure that everything is correct and report the numbers to your authorities. Your goal is to reach a level where even your accounting is automated as part of your store factory, but before all technical pieces of the puzzle are there you will need to perform manual work. The good thing is that a big chunk of this manual work can be done by someone else.

GET HELP WITH YOUR ACCOUNTING

If you are using any online service for your accounting it is easy to get help from someone else to assist with the manual work. Most services have a user management feature, where you can add additional users for your company or invite specific users from an accounting firm. And by sending all your papers by email either to your accounting firm, or by the email-to-accounting-feature of some online services, your manual work can be limited to ensuring that you have sent all your receipts and invoices to the correct email address.

To hire an accounting firm can feel like an expensive expense initially, but it is really a headache that is much worth getting rid of. And by searching for an accounting firm or an individual who can help you with these things online, you can help realising someone else's dream of reaching a life as a digital nomad. To manage the accounting for an e-commerce operation in the startup phase such as described in this book should not have to take more than 2-3 hours per month for a good accountant.

Once you have agreed with a firm or an individual, invite this person to your online accounting service by adding an account with their email adress in the users section of the services settings. After this, agree on routines for your work together and write those down in a simple operation procedure document. This document will help you to figure out a lot of things in advance and in that way avoid unnecessary costs in long phone calls and extra hours charged by your new consultant.

Your operation procedure document should contain:

• A definition of what you expect the consultant/accountant to help you with.

• Expected effort, for example, to do the accounting once per month or once per week.

• The deadlines each month when you should have sent all material for the last month's transactions, and which day the accounting should be expected to be updated.

• Who is responsible for the ongoing reporting to tax authorities.

• Expected number of documents (invoices, receipts etc) that should be handled every month.

• How to deal with automatically generated material and which ones should be expected each month. For example, from Shopify, Stripe and your bank.

• How you practically handle recipes and expenses. How you, for example, markup if an invoice was paid with the company money or if it should be reimbursed to you.

Use the operation procedure as a living document updated as your joint work develops. In this way, you will have an easier way replacing the accountant if needed, and the one you hire will also feel more confident there is a document to lean on if anything is unclear.

ROUTINES

Accounting is something that easily can end up at the bottom of the todo list, far from what one want to spend time with on a Sunday afternoon. Therefore let routines be in control, no matter if it is just to check that an automatic accounting works, to check in on what someone else did to the numbers, or to collect material, import them into an accounting software and actually book every transaction one by one.

A manageable routing for your paperwork need not be more difficult than this:

• Each time you buy something, immediately import the receipt into your accounting software or service.

• The first Tuesday of each month, go through the accounting from last months and check that everything is updated and under control.

• Every time after you finish your Saturday run, check in on your sales numbers in the accounting (not only in Shopify).

Make sure the routines you set up are as close to your everyday chores as possible. If you set up your routines when maybe they will compete with pleasures, chances are much higher that they will be postponed.

Tips! Get an app that encourages and allows you to follow up on your routines. They work both for making sure that you put those 30 minutes into guitar practice each day, and that you go through your accounting every week.

Habitify (https://habitify.me/) is such an app for your smartphone.

REAL LIFE ACCOUNTING

Even if your goal is to have all accounting happen automatically, know what goes on behind those automatic processes. Also, before you have it all automated, you must take care of or outsource it yourself. Below are examples of how your accounting can look like, based roughly on how I manage my own.

The accounting rules will differ from country to country, but the material you need will be the same everywhere.

Every month you must book the transactions for:
- Sales from Shopify.
- Transfer of funds from Stripe to your bank.
- Fees from Stripe.

Except for these, you will also have invoices coming in from Shopify, Facebook, Google and your other suppliers you need to book as well.

Sales from Shopify
Export a sales report from Shopify that covers last month's sales. You will find the report under *Analytics -> Reports -> Financies -> Finances summary.*
Use this as basis for your accounting regarding sold goods.

Transfer of funds from Stripe to your bank
Export a transaction report from Stripe that covers last month's payments. You will find the report under *Balance -> Payouts (filter = aktuell månad) -> Export.*

The report will be exported in CSV-format. Download the report, open it in your spreadsheet application and export it as PDF. This way you can upload the document directly to your accounting software.

Fees from Stripe

Export a report for the fees from Stripe directly from their website. You will find the report Tax Invoice under *Business settings -> Documents*.

Book the invoice as paid directly from the Stripe account, since the fee has been deducted automatically from the funds transferred to you.

TO RUN YOUR COMPANY

Now that you have your store factory in place, with everything from warehouse and e-commerce platform and accounting, it is time to operate it. I hope you have cheated and received your first orders already, but for sake of formality let's go through what you should now spend your time doing. And what you shouldn't spend time doing.

MARKETING

To get your message out there to more people is the sole reason we have spent so much time and energy to make you free from the operative tasks in your location independent business. In this area you should put most of your time as an e-commercing digital nomad. No matter if you write posts on Instagram and buy ads from Google AdWords yourself or if you hire someone to do it for you, this is what you should spend your energy doing.

Try to build structure for your marketing activities. Try out a lot of format and methods, but note their actual results. As with most things, marketing is a game of measuring, adjusting and measuring again. Make things easy on yourself using the tools already available to you, or quickly create your own overviews in Numbers or Excel if you don't feel comfortable with the complexity of existing tools. Within services like Google AdWords you can easily get an overview of how your campaigns are doing and compare which ones that gave the best results. Organic traffic coming from things like adding a photo of a product on Instagram or posting a short video can be harder to follow up with statistics. In those cases, it's better to keep things simple and just write down statistics in a spreadsheet of how many followers you had before and after your activity and if it resulted in any additional sales. Once you find something that works, adjust, do more of it and measure again.

Also add routines for the marketing into your daily

life. Run a simple post on Instagram every Tuesday and Thursday and publish something bigger on Fridays. Take the chance to adjust your rolling ads at the same time. Social media likes continuity and recurring interactions, paid ads like you have control over where and how the money is spent.

DEVELOPMENT

In the middle of all your expected success with orders that keep flowing in marketing campaigns that result in lots of interactions, it's hard to keep your head clear about where you are heading.

Before you even start your company, put an event in your calendar on a day six months from now. Call it "Analysis of my company" and when you reach that date, get yourself to a nice café with a piece of paper and a pen and write down how things have developed the last six months, and how you want it to proceed for the next half year. Force yourself to not sit still with your company.

Pride is a good component to use in one's entrepreneurship, Especially in relation to what we have talked about before - to find a calling and build a company around it. But be careful so the pride doesn't evolve into stubbornness. Most successful companies started as an idea adjusted so heavily during the journey of the company it can hardly be the same idea when the success eventually came. Your calling will be to define the area you want to work within, but don't be afraid to broaden yourself or change direction and business model of your company if you don't get the traction you are looking for.

When you have your moment of analysing how your company is doing, put your pride aside. During your board meetings you should be all about the business inside the walls you set out for yourself when you started the company, and think about ways to improve or change your operations. But during the time of reflection, think outside any walls you might have. Feel what would happen if you would just tare them down, or change the direction of your company completely.

When your business is ticking you will not have to do any big changes and suddenly change a working setup, but play with it in your mind anyway - what happens if our main selling product suddenly stops being interesting to our customers? Focus your development to broaden your business, make it more sustainable and lessen your dependency on single products and single markets. The world will inevitably change and it is better to have thought about the change a few steps ahead, so you know how to act once it does.

Tips! Create a note in your phone with the name "Development ideas" and let your fantasy fill it with ideas about how you could develop your company even between those half-yearly sessions at the café. That way you can quickly put an idea aside in that note and get back to focus on the operations at hand, and still not forget it until your next session of analysis.

CUSTOMER RELATIONS

As a digital nomad, customer relations are a double-edged sword. On one hand, it is something that you must use to effectively build up your following, loyal customers and reputation as an e-commerce stop. At the same time too many customer interactions can mess up your ambitions of acquiring freedom as a digital nomad. Luckily it is possible to plan for this and design your store factory so you find your balance on that sword's edge that makes both your customers happy and your digital nomadship successful.

Generally, you should strive to personally connect with your customers. With personal, I mean that the tone and way you communicate with your customers should be personal. Even if your e-commerce store is a giant in your field, people will like relaxed interactions with a real name on the other side.

To communicate with your customers is also important, not only to learn what you must improve in your operation, but also to inject happiness and joy into your own work situation. If you are never exposed to the interactions between your company and its customers, you will quickly become very theoretical in how you run your business, or even worse tire of it completely. This is especially true when working as a digital nomad and don't meet customers and colleagues in your company physically every day.

As we have talked about earlier, it is nevertheless

important that you don't put yourself in the middle of the flow of operations of your business, so your contacts with a customer are required for the operations to not stop. You need to design your flows, so you are not required to be in there, but have all the possibilities to jump in if you like to.

The optimal way of dealing with customer interactions is that you initiate contact yourself. Choose a customer from last week and write them a short email and simply ask them how the experience of shopping with you was. Or thank a profile on Instagram personally when they share a photo of your product. Compared to being the point of contact only when something goes wrong, this will give you lots of positive energy instead of negative.

For the routine interactions that are needed, prioritise automating them or outsourcing them. Make sure that returns are handled by your warehouse supplier and that an automatic email is always sent a week after the customer has received their order, as we discussed in the chapter about your store factory earlier.

As for the other parts of your operations, you can also for your customer interactions set up routines so they actually get done, until they become a natural part of your everyday work. Decide on a day of the week when you initiate customer contacts and spend half an hour sending away a few emails that day. Answer and follow up as the replies come back. Repeat next week. Also don't be afraid to send out discount codes or other gifts to your existing customers, they are a lot closer to buying something more from you than any person you had nothing to do with before.

WHAT YOU HAVE LEARNED

You have now learned the practical basics of how to start your own e-commerce business, that you can run from anywhere in the world. From finding your calling to start something that you can be passionate about, to practical advice about how you should think about formulating your business idea. *I will sell X to Y and will succeed because of Z.* We have also talked about how you find others products and how you can create your own. And how you can think to package these into something that your customers might want to buy. How you interact with factories in China via Alibaba or how you can think about manufacturing your own product and still be location independent. We have also talked about how to think product even when selling services, so you set things up for scaling up already from the start.

From idea and product we have touched upon both specific tips and guides to how you shape your own business. We have discussed how you can think about incorporation options, how to come up with a name and how to get all the practical details in place already from start with e-mail and cloud services. As a digital nomad, we are most often considered a one-man-show, but we have gone through how you can build a virtual organisation for your company that will boost your digital nomadship, not feather you to the ground.

You have also learned the practical steps of actually setting up a Shopify store and getting everything from accounting to product descriptions in order. We have talked about which marketing channels to bet on and how they are set up. How to constantly adjust the experience of shopping with you and lots and lots of tips about how you can make your e-commerce business a success.

To learn more and continue to be inspired about your life as a digital nomad, I recommend these three things:

1.   Read *The 4-hour Workweek* by Tim Ferris.

2.   Register for the Shopify Academy and get inspired by their online courses.

3.   Just do it! Despite all the detailed tips and advice I have given throughout this book, they are of no use unless you start somewhere. So start already today. Begin with a small project on the side while you continue your day-job, or go all the way and revolutionise the world!

THANKS TO YOU

I want to take the opportunity to thank you for having read this book. I hope it has given you valuable insights and more importantly a lot of inspiration for your journey towards becoming a digital nomad. No matter if your plan is to work from a kitchen table in Gothenburg or from a sun bed in Thailand.

Please let me know how things are going with your specific digital nomad project!

You can reach me at erik@karlberg.org or on most social media via @erikkarlberg. More information about this book and my other projects and thoughts can be found at https://erikkarlberg.com/.

Also my e-commerce agency Smond builds e-commerce websites and solutions using Shopify, so if you need help taking things to the next level – let me know at erik@smond.se!

Best of luck!

Erik Karlberg

9 789198 448368